Bad Ha

MW00951465

This book is a series of poems from Jonathan Muhiudeen's sailing experience. The poems in the book are just poems; they are not about anyone, anyplace or incident. Any resemblance to any person, place or written work is purely coincidental. The reader should not consider this book anything other than a work of literature.

Photos by Jonathan Muhiudeen, Wikipedia , Google Earth and pexels.com, tOrange.biz

First Printing, 2015,
ISBN -13: 978-1516859597
ISBN -10: 1516859596

CreateSpace Independent Publishing Platform, North Charleston, SC

Publisher Jonathan Muhiudeen
Jonathan.saltintherainbow@gmail.com
www.facebook.com/jonathanpoems

Publisher's Cataloging-in-Publication data.
A title of a book: Bad Habits - Sailing Poetry by Jonathan Muhiudeen.

BISAC: POE000000 POETRY / General

This book is dedicated to

The Members of

The Royal Selangor Yacht Club,

Malaysia

Introduction:

I learnt to sail at the Royal Selangor Yacht Club (RSYC); it became my home from home.

From there I sailed on boats of all shapes and sizes; from old 100 foot classics to 14 foot carbon fiber dinghies. I raced in many races and also created races. It was from the RSYC that I launched *my round the world sailing adventure*. The sailing community has given me many close friends and a berth to drink and eat in yacht clubs everywhere.

This book is dedicated to the RSYC, as she is called, its members; to the staff, to the sailing members and to the non-sailing members - all those wonderful people.

RSYC sits in the Klang River estuary, just 3 degrees north of the equator, half way up the Straits of Malacca. It's hot, has warm water, light winds, strong currents and strong line squalls. I started to sail where you could swim off the transom; eat the seafood you caught; or anchor for the night and just have fun without any hard danger. It was a great place to learn to sail as you could survive the mistakes, that we all make from going hard aground.. getting lost.. having too much sail up..falling off the boat. LOL at the memories. It was also great, as there were no coastguard or boat yards, we just had to look after each other and be independent.

This is what RSYC looked like when I started sailing in the early 80's; note the 18 feet tidal difference at the club's dock.

I started to jot down my thoughts, after I wrote the book about my circumnavigation, called "Salt in the Rainbow", and from those thoughts, came this book.

I hope you all enjoy it, my suggestion is to read a couple of poems at a time, and then come back when you have a moment.

Fair winds,

Jonathan Muhiudeen
Jonathan.saltintherainbow@gmail.com

Index

Traveler

I would rather gaze upon a snow capped range of
mountains
than the Mona Lisa

I would rather watch the sun rise over stormy water
than a movie

I would rather sit around a campfire with friends
than meet with the President

I would rather eat fruit on a trail
than eat at a 5 star restaurant

I would rather be by myself
than in a crowd of strangers

But most of all I rather be with Thee.

Salt in the Rainbow

Salt

is in my blood

is in my tears

is in my past

and my future

It's the salt on ships

it's the salt in the sea

it's the salt in the rainbow

that it's in our blood

that splices you to me

and when I lie asleep

I dream of you

I see salt in the rainbow

that comes from you

Ripples of the sun,

off the sea

the horizon calling me

warm wind is blowing

it's time to set a course, and go and be free.

Dreamers, Doers and Donners

The journey

around the world

Does not start with the first step

does not stop when you complete

The journey

starts with a dream

a crazy dream

one of the wild crazy dreams

to dream to be free

to travel

to follow

the setting sun

right around the world

you start as a dreamer

then become a doer

then a donner

Dreamer, Doer, Donner

The 3 D's of life

But when you are old

and you cannot do

The donner

becomes a dreamer

but dreams of

being done

Life is a circle

a golden DDD circle

Dreamer Doer Donner

Dah Di Dit

Dah Di Dit

Dah Di Dit.

Ocean Love

Ocean

hold me tight

like a long lost lover

Hold me tight

with that magic spell

That you captured me

a long time ago

Ocean

hold me tight

like a long lost lover

with your soothing waves

and kiss my life

When you press that salt water

to my heart

I see a world apart

a multicolored world

where life thrives

I give my heart and soul to you

and I will always be free.

Log entry: Australia

Sometimes it happens

and it's suddenly worth

all the pain,

worry

money

Crystal clear Night,

stars like seafarers from all times are overhead.

Ocean everywhere

gentle waves

our wake glowing in the gentle darkness

as we move

as only a monohull can

Dolphins dart around the bow

as music and black label is consumed

Their squeaks can be heard

along with the clicks and ticks

of the boats heartbeat

Yes sometimes it happens

and

makes it all worth it.

113nm to go to next way point.

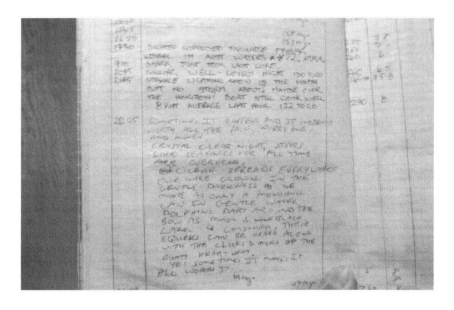

Double

I want to sail

I want to travel

from this life

that holds me

I want to be free

not from

but to be

I want that gentle breeze

that sunlight

that air

that crisp wavy horizon

To be free

to roam

where there are no roads

no paths

To take

not the lesser path but

where there are no paths

I want to be free

and be with you

before I turn to rust

before I can't show you

that special place

Do you feel the same

and with each night

let's love and dream

it's easy

I have someone

so do you

Is it not too late

to seek

that dream

it's blowing in the wind

and when we go

We will be free.

Blues for the Ocean

The cradle of life is dying

Teardrops of the Ocean

salt

fall

silently

within the Ocean

The Ocean is dying

for us all to see

Acidification

pollution

plasticifaction

rape

genocide

The cradle of life is dying

the blue bells toll

they toll

they toll

But we humans can't hear

because we are already dead

Just

we don't know it yet.

Champagne sailing

We often wonder

where

when

we will get to Champagne sail

Champagne sailing is where everything goes right

from the sun to the moon

from the wave to the breeze

from the fish to the mammals

from movement to movement

Champagne sailing is not very common

but enough

to keep us going

Night Champagne sailing

is special

Night sailing is special

There sounds and movement

sounds that that kiss you

Not that sound of

rumble of a breaking wave

not that sound

of salt water turning into ice before shattering on deck

not that sound

that a flying fish makes as they land on deck

or a sea bird crashing into your sails

or cry

All hands on deck

Champagne night sailing

is like great sex

it's rhythmic

it's gentle

it's lasting

it's natural

We sail across those Oceans

those seas

those bays

so we can experience Champagne sailing

because we believe it's always like that.

Like life

champagne sailing does exists

not just at sea

but in my dreams.

The flying fish with a golden trident

The flying fish
hated/fears (it's the same)
all those that chased him

Tuna,
Mackerel
Wahoo
even the bloody birds

But the one this flying fish
hates/fears (it's the same)
the most is
the Mahi Mahi

The Mahi Mahi
it is so cocky that you have to say his name twice
it is so cocky that it does not just have one color
no, everything has to be super-duper
it not just swims
but pretends to fly too

So one day

the Mahi Mahi was chasing

the flying fish

all day

over the Ocean

across the sky

(well not all the way, just a little bit, but the flying fish

didn't know that)

That night,

the flying fish went to see

Poseidon

and asked

can I borrow

your golden trident?

I promise to return it

After,

I skewer that Mahi Mahi

who has been chasing me

all day

over the Ocean

across the sky

(well not all the way across the sky, just a little bit, but the flying fish didn't know that)

Poseidon

said

but it's too big

And the flying fish said

I'll try

He laughed

as only a sea god can

and took the

Very

very

tip of his Trident

and made

a small

trident

for the flying fish

With that the flying fish

sailed around the world

and was never

afraid again.

So when you see flying fish

skim across the Ocean

across your bow

keep a look out

for the one with the golden trident,

and say "Hi" for me.

(Just don't tell the flying fish

that the trident is

too small

to kill a Mahi Mahi

but the Mahi Mahi

doesn't know that.)

My friend

My friend,

At the end of time
it's you I got to know
there is no going back

I wouldn't change a thing
even if I could

But if I could
I would do it all over

Our lives together
across the sea
we are the setting sun off the sea
we are the warm wind blowing
the flying fish skimming across the bow
that salt
that is in our rainbow
we are forever

Dangerous things

Danger is

was

and ought to be

an art

or stylish

Doing dangerous things

take style

doing dangerous things

takes a kind of person

a stylish person

But doing dangerous things

many times are not as it looks

No

dangerous things are safer than

doing everyday things

Doing it is better than

not doing it

Doing dangerous things is

better than not doing it..

If you are a stylish kind

Danger is

was and

will always

be a stylish thing

Cliff

sky

cave

rock face

summit

ice

empty quarter

diving

black diamond

formula 1

lime green Kawasaki

Or just dancing

in the shower

naked

alone

Because. ..

it's there.

<u>Night Watch</u>

I deep asleep

a wet dripping hand

shakes me

from that warm, safe bed.

"its 3am

your're on"

it says to me

yawning

blinking

disbelieving

Clothes

waterproofs

harness

boots

gloves

tea

Another blink

quick look at the chart

A deep breath

feet on the ladder

hatch open

darkness, cold and rain pours in,

and..the roar of the waves.

Yes I'm on.

City reef

Why are all bars alike

busy in the middle

quiet on the edge

like a reef in the middle of nowhere

attended by all the wrong fish

The no good tasting fish are close in

sharks outside them

Then in the big hazy blue

there the real kings of fish live

Mahi-mahi, Wahoo, Yellowfin

their names say it all

speed, elegance, power and more speed

They go where they please

but still they need to eat

so like the bar flies

they coast in and out

to the reef

Frightened of the busyness

but dare not to stray too far

sometimes they slow down enough to see what goes on

Ask any Groupa

the Groupa sees it all

but they never go anywhere

let alone anyplace

What a life

just sitting on the bar

watching, waiting for life to drift by

Nothing like the pelagic boys,

moving so fast that

everything except their prey

escapes them

its even more apparent

when you get into the car park outside

True reflection

of the nature of the fish

Fast, sleek

slow, steady

boring, practical

BM's, Merc

Volvo, Protons

Funnily enough

like fast fish

they are the same color

same family

Funnily enough

they have to do the same thing

same speed limits

same bullshit

more in others than some

I suppose

that it says it all.

Gale

A gale

brings fear to every sailor's heart

shakes to the limbs

trembles to the knees

Gale is more than a name

more than a term

More than a nightmare

gale sucks out my fear from

my steel

my soul

my pores

But at night

strangely at night

gale fear is easier at night

where darkness hides gale's ways

and the others

the other's eyes

But at dawn...

light the color of guns light

try to see

foam spat in your eyes

chaos, fear

and the waves

Waves like mountains

mountains with blinding foam

with sudden judo throws

karate chops

deafening attacking roars

Even on a calm day lying in bed

I can hear

the attacking roars but...

But not this day

busyness in happiness

busyness in simple flat white sheets

busyness in not putting to sea.

She

She came around the corner

with such grace

That gentle movement

those curves

those lines

Lust rushes

through my body

unfaithful thoughts

rush through my

body

mind

and soul

She slides pass me

and everyman

stares

She slides pass

knowing

that she has our attention

And that she will

own our love

but outlive

us all

And then excite a new generation

of wooden ships lovers.

Bad Habits

Have to confess

that I have bad habits

ok, one very, very

bad habit

The habit

to want

to sail across the sea

The holy three

Pacific

Atlantic

Indian

Big Blue

the Pond

monsoon

Now, not all is bad

as I don't have

the habit

to want

to sail across

the Bering strait

or Drakes Passage

on an angry day

Or chase

any hurricane

any where

any time

any place

any hemisphere

even if they don't call it

a Hurricane.

Is it my age

maturity

or the scars

on my left wrist

or the PTSD

or plain fear

From that wrong forecast

of a hurricane

that was not supposed to happen

long ago

that winter

that wrong forecast

So I have bad habits

but not

anywhere

any time

any sea.

So now,

I sail

when I see flying fish

as they know

When not to go

when

it is too cold

too calm

too windy

To be truthful
they are pretty smart
for a fish.

Big Blue

It's that big one
that's half the world
that rolling surfing
Pacific Ocean called
Big Blue.

You can spend weeks
on a tack
and everyday
is perfect
on the Big Blue

Steady breeze
warm nights
everything you
ever wanted
in an Ocean
is in the Big Blue

Crossing the Big Blue
is scary

no turning back

no use calling Mum

no

you're on your own

everything you ever wanted

in an Ocean

That Big Blue.

My Brother

You're my brother

I have a feeling that
I know in my heart
although
we have just met
you're my brother

It's the salt
in our veins
in our traditions
that bonds us

Let's be castaways
drift
across the sea
sailing away
under the sun and stars
and be free

There is a change

a monsoon change

Let's follow

our history

our path

our father's

on the

monsoon change

Follow the

monsoon wind

across the sea

And not get old.

Samudra (The Ocean)

Samsara

Samudra

That Ocean

that island

that sea

that tide

that ebb

that flood

Of my dreams

where Ocean waves

come to a black beach

over crystal water

from Samudra

that meeting of the sea

Misty morning

orange dawn

gentle

slow

jasmin breaths

peace
emptiness
beyond happiness
the void
the end
is the beginning
is found everywhere

Samudra.

Green Light Red Light

Green on my right

red on my left

The lights steady

to show that I

am on the move

Again

yes again

White is my tail

yellow my tow

blinking blue means police

Blinking white can mean some many things

from a star above

to rocks below

Not all lights

are born equal

not all are danger

But not all are friends

At night

be safe

keep watch

over all those

lights

till dawn comes

And then

you know

Boat Yard Blues

She lay there
forgotten

Many years
of children's feet
running on her deck

Many years
of laughter
of parties
of love
of just sailing

She did her duty
protected
them

Took the hits
from bad mistakes
not of hers
both at sea

and ashore

Now she lies

forgotten

and cursed

when the yard bill comes.

She lays there

forgotten

but she can't move on

As

she won't be given

a second life

till he gets all his money back

which will never happen

Just the boat yard blues.

Laluan (Passage)

It is you I got to know

this passage

across the sea

across the sky

across the rainbow

We see eye to eye

this world

this Ocean

this blessed place

we call home

Across the deck

Across the helm

Across the cardinals

It's you I got to know

till the end of time

This band of brothers

who's salt flow thru

thru this passage

thru the sea

thru this time

thru us

It's you I got to know

Thank you.

Mother Ocean

From us

who use the Ocean

Sailors

swimmers

beach lovers

fisherman

surfers

divers

those who just watch the waves

Children who run up and down

the beach

chased by the waves

screaming in delight

Happy Ocean day, everyone

Cold Change

Cold wind

soothes my wounds

A cold change

is coming

a cold front

is in the air

The thermometer

and the barometer

are dropping

like a stone

Tears flow

never to return

frozen in time

in the cold wind

The wind heralds

it's time to tack

it's time to gybe

Time to feel

The

The change in my heart.

Clouds

I love the clouds outside my boat

rushing past

misty

solid

puffy

reflective

opaque

I love clouds as they develop

bulging

gaping

rolling

indented

swirling

I love the clouds as they leave the island tops clear

softness

penetrated by hardness

flowing

over stillness

smoothness

sliding over jaggedness

I love clouds

above my boat

and sex.

Delivery

Dawn flight

orange horizon

purple haze

Ice on the window

snow on the ground

Distance place flash by

all in the night

Heathrow, Paris, Rome

All in the night

a delivery

awaits me

to cross an

Ocean

to cross a sea

Distance place flash by

all in the night.

WTF is that?

You know you are old

when you love

J boats

12 meters

bloopers peels

and you were excited

to go over 10 kts

You know you are old

when you sit in the RIB

on the line

trying to work out

WTF Is that?

Pulled by a kite

and I don't mean a spinnaker

it has no rudder

it has a foil

somehow connected

to the person

I think is standing

To say it is uncomfortable

is an understatement

I mean

where is the

beer cooler?

or seats

or shelter

You know you are old

when you expect

the boat you are on

to sail in any conditions

in any directions

just like us

But perhaps

only sailing in winds under 25 kts

but sailing at 30 kts in total silence

without too much chop

is not youth

just smart.

Spinnaker

It's a beat

wind on the nose

freezing cold

Pitching

rolling

yawing

and yes

fucking heeling

up on the rail

wind in the eye

scanning for the mark

Spin pole up

set and gybe

they cry in greek

or was it latin

as we fly

Men

tired men

pulling, shoving swearing

a bag along the deck

waves crashing over them

Freezing

pitching

rolling

yawing

and now bucking

FREE THE GUY

AND THE FUCKING SHEET

we shout

faces wet

eyes stinging

throat dry

backs aching

the pole skinning

our knuckles

banging our heads

hit our shins

tears our palms

struggling to stand

COMING UP......

STAND BY...they cry

GO GO GO GO

we hear

Jumping high

hand over hand

up the halyard

pulling fast

using our weight

our dead tired weight

pulling

pumping

shouts

and cries

rattle of the pawls

metal on metal

groan on groan

oath upon oath

praying

LET IT BE GOOD

bang

The whole boat shudders

rolls over and yaws

life line blur

blood on deck

PULL

COME ON *FUCKING* PULL

PULL

Crack and bang and roar

and the spin FILLS

We are on our way

It's time for a beer

If the skipper did not forget them again.

The Path

Blinded by mortality

We can't see the path
well beaten
by a hand greater than I
that leads to the Ocean

Step by step
your path that you
choose

Step by step
an illusion of logic and choice
whatever you chose
you will end up on
the path to God's country

Far from the manicured suburbia
far from nature's death
far from the diseased man's world

lies the path to God's country

It's a lie that all roads lead to Rome

it's a man's futile vanity

for as we all know

That all roads lead to God's Country

to the Ocean

to the sea.

Wild places

I love to go and wander

along

the snowy mountain tops

the wind swept plains

the raging river

the dark caves

and the sleepless sea

Wandering

visiting

longing it

Yes, I love to go and wander

where my spirit is free

and my soul is honest

Yes Wander

the air is clear

my eyes are happy

I love to go wander

through

the valleys

the glacier cracks

the dark canals

the city alleys

Wander

Visiting

Loving it

Most of all,

needing it.

Zip Code

Why is it that I cannot remember my zip code

it's not that I don't use it

nor even get asked about it

Maybe my zip code changes

like a season

5 digit means winter

alphabetical means summer

3 digits means that I am lost

And nine digits

that I am home

at home my zip

is more than a zip

no it's my number.

Clear Water Anchorage

You know
when the water is clear
there is a shadow on the seabed
a shadow under your boat

You can see your shadow
there too
on that white sandy floor

You can't tell the depth
jump off the side
expecting to hit the sandy bottom

But keep on going down
and down
in the clear clear warm water
small bubbles following you down

Fish looking at you in surprise
saying welcome back
in my dreams.

Uncle Wayne

The little boy looked up and squinted his eyes

in the dying but bright sun

to look at his father

He reached up and grabbed his hand

as they walked down the beach

feeling the warmth strength of this familiar loving hand

The evening cool slowly crept into the day

they walked slowly down the beach, hand in hand

the boy's uncle shouted

"Those seagulls are like rats"

"like rats"

The boy asked "Why are they like rats?"

he replied as he started to run down the beach waving his

hands

"Because they eat everything and poop on my boat"

The sea gulls that were standing on the beach

facing the wind

with one leg tucked up for warmth

minding their own business

Took off effortlessly into the breeze, in waves, crying

"mine, mine, mine, mine"

as the uncle ran close to them

on their beach

The boy lets go of his father's hand

and ran after him, shouting

"Shoo Shoo"

waving his all his arms at the seagulls.

The uncle ran on the beach until he was tired

dropped into the sand, which was not very far

his hands breaking the warm sand's crust,

he felt the cool moist sand just below the warm crust

the day's stress flowed out of him

The little boy caught up with his uncle and dropped into

the sand next to him

they both lay there

as the sun slowly dipped into the sea

As it was

as it is

as is time immemorial

The little boy stood up and took his father's hand and

walked home to have dinner

his uncle just laid there

his hair grey from the salt of the sea

and watched the day pass, saying to himself

"Like rats".

Sailing Alone

Alone
solo
singlehanded
has its privileges

No one above you
no one below you

It's a special place
that silence
that rare space
that calm

It's special to sail alone

Whenswe were younger
we sailed drunken
beer in both hands
and one for the ship
Odin steered
Poseidon navigated

Tangaroa trimmed

youth served

Now we sail alone

with just the

Wind

Waves

And Thee.

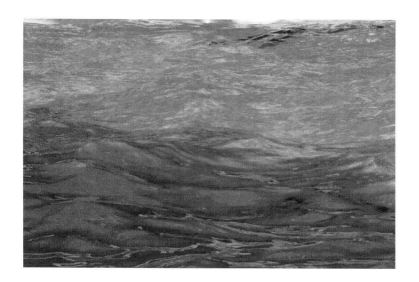

Rendezvous

Across the starry night

along the travelers way

a rendezvous

awaits me

Along the traveler's way

death has eluded me

but awaits me

along the travelers way

At my exit interview

where I will be awarded

the death certificate

I will leave all my

life, liberty and pursuit of happiness

At the end of the travelers way

with nothing but memories, scars and laughter

at the exit interview

they will ask

"did you have fun"

I hope to say

thank you

for this wonderful gift

called life

That took me across that starry night

along that traveler's way.

GO, BEFORE IT IS TOO LATE

Warna ku   (Your color)

It's the bright gold

off the deep blue

restless sea

It's the silver sheen

off the snow

in the mountain

It's the red flash

of a humming bird

wings

flying

It's the glitter of

a stream

in the forest

It's the light

in your eye

over a fireplace

It is all light

that flashes through

my mind

When I think of you.

Wake

Our past and future is interwoven

like a wake

between life and death

between bow and stern

our wakes are interwoven

We race through life

you hold me in the palm of your hand

with wind in my ears

your tears stain my heart

while it flies free

Our passage through time

down the staircase of darkness,

from the bow to the stern

into the velvet

Salt in our future

Salt in our past

Salt in our blood

Salt in our tears

Noise in a crowded room
light filtering in
bringing in your face
across the world
into my heart

Salty tears flow
thankful for the journey

Till me meet again
sleep well

Dawn is coming.

Choices

You get to choose your memories

you choose well and you will be happy

you choose badly and you will be bitter

It's your memories

it's your choice

it's your happiness

People who have hurt you

do not have the right

to be in your memory

Don't let them

twist you

Don't choose bitterness

Choose to be Happy

Jonathan Muhiudeen lives in the San Francisco Bay area.

He has circumnavigated the globe under sail and has published a book about the trip called "Salt in the Rainbow" which is available from online book shops.

He writes poems when thinks of them, mostly lying in his bunk before dawn.

You can find him at:
www.facebook.com/saltintherainbow
www.facebook.com/jonathanpoems

or contact him at:
jonathan.saltintherainbow@gmail.com

Other books by Jonathan

Salt in the Rainbow

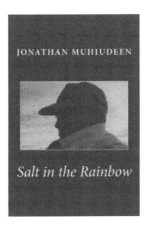

Poems from the Stream

Available online at Amazon as a book or an ebook

Made in the USA
San Bernardino, CA
15 February 2017